LIFE
SKILLS

Sir William Turner
Learning Resource Centre
Redcar & Cleveland College

REDCAR &
CLEVELAND
COLLEGE

LIBRARY

www.heinemann.co.uk/library

Visit our website to find out more information about **Heinemann Library** books.

To order:

☎ Phone 44 (0) 1865 888066

▤ Send a fax to 44 (0) 1865 314091

🖥 Visit the Heinemann Bookshop at www.heinemann.co.uk/library to browse our catalogue and order online.

Heinemann Library is an imprint of Pearson Education Limited, a company incorporated in England and Wales having its registered office at Edinburgh Gate, Harlow, Essex, CM20 2JE – Registered company number: 00872828

"Heinemann" is a registered trademark of Pearson Education Limited.

Edited by Pollyanna Poulter
Designed by Philippa Jenkins and Hart MacLeod
Original illustrations © Pearson Education Limited by Clare Elsom
Picture research by Elizabeth Alexander and Maria Joannou
Production by Alison Parsons
Originated by Modern Age Repro House Ltd.
Printed and bound in China by South China Printing Company Ltd.

ISBN 978 0 431112 40 4 (hardback)
13 12 11 10 09
10 9 8 7 6 5 4 3 2 1

British Library Cataloguing-in-Publication Data
Mack, Jim
Be a great babysitter! - (Life skills)
1. Babysitting - Juvenile literature
I. Title
649.1'0248
A full catalogue record for this book is available from the British Library.

Acknowledgements
We would like to thank the following for permission to reproduce photographs: © Alamy: pp. **4** (David L. Moore), **14** (Corbis Premium RF/ Colorblind), **22** (Jupiterimages/Comstock Images), **36** (Sally and Richard Greenhill), **38** (Avatra images), **46** (Angela Hampton Picture Library); © Corbis: p. **16** (Michael N. Paras); © Getty Images: pp. **7** (Aurora/Dennis Welsh), **26** (Digital Vision), **43** (Iconica/Camille Tokerud), **49** (Photonica/Betsie Van Der Meer); © Istockphoto: p. **29** (Mike Panic); © Masterfile: pp. **21** (Mark Tomalty), **31** (Chad Johnston), **32** (Tom Feiler); © Pearson Education Ltd: p. **44** (Jules Selmes); © Photolibrary: p. **41** (Hurewitz Creative); © Punchstock: p. **19** (Digital Vision); © Rex Features: p. **12** (Burger/Phanie); © Topham Picturepoint: p. **9** (Bob Daemmrich/The Image Works).

Cover photograph of woman playing with a baby reproduced with permission of © 2008 Masterfile Corporation (Norbert Schäfer).

We would like to thank Kate Madden for her invaluable help in the preparation of this book.

Every effort has been made to contact copyright holders of material reproduced in this book. Any omissions will be rectified in subsequent printings if notice is given to the Publishers.

Contents

Some words are printed in bold, **like this**. You can find out what they mean by looking in the glossary.

Why Babysitting?

If you see yourself as one day working with young children, babysitting is the best place to start gaining experience and developing business skills. If you are not ready to pursue a career just yet, even babysitting for close family members is a fantastic way to learn responsibility and gain useful skills.

More Than a Job

An important reason to have a job is to make money. Babysitting can be a **lucrative** side job. But to be truly successful, you must first enjoy being with children and want to take care of them to the best of your ability.

Becoming a babysitter is great experience to have if one day you want to be a nanny, childcare worker,

Finding a job takes some effort. Explore all your options. Ask friends and relatives for advice, as well as looking in your local paper for any job advertisements or listings.

or even a teacher. Babysitting will also help you develop your social skills and become a good leader, which will give you the confidence to pursue any career.

Getting it Right

It is important not to be stressed or upset while babysitting. If you're not comfortable with a situation, a child's safety could be at risk, so only babysit if you can totally focus on the children without distraction from other areas of your life. If a child has an accident or makes a mess, make sure they are not injured and calmly help them clean it up. Try to stay calm and continue to stay focused on providing supervision.

Is it for you?

Even though half of the word babysitting is "sitting," don't expect to show up and sit around for a couple of hours! It is not that simple. Babysitters are in charge of the safety of as many children as they have been employed to watch. When parents leave their child in your care, that child's life is in your hands. If you are not prepared for that kind of responsibility, or if you are not that enthusiastic about caring for children, then babysitting may not be the right job for you.

A babysitter is expected to take charge and make mature decisions. But being in charge does not mean you cannot play with the children – in fact, half the job will be playing with them. You want to become closer with the children, create a welcoming environment, and gain their trust, but you need to be more than just their friend. Remember, you are there to watch them, not **mould** them. A babysitter is a role model for children, so be a good influence. You will gain the trust of children and parents alike by being responsible and reliable.

Babysitting can be a very fulfilling experience. You will learn a lot about children – and a lot about yourself.

DID YOU KNOW?

The term "babysitter" was first used, and first appeared in print, in 1937. Between 1945 and 1947 the term "baby-sit" began being used. World War II took place between the years 1939 and 1945. It is possible that babysitting became common practice during the war. This could have been as a result of women needing extra help to care for their families while their husbands were away at war.

Starting Out

Babysitting may sound like an easy job, but it can be just as hard as any other job. Whether it is for one night or multiple nights, a babysitter is expected to care for children in the same way as a parent. The job of babysitting is extremely important to parents. The lives of their children are in the hands of the babysitter, so they look for someone they can trust and have faith in.

ARE YOU QUALIFIED?

Most parents rely on **referrals** from other parents when searching for a babysitter. They will often consult other parents they know for a **reference** when they are looking for someone to employ. Having babysitting experience is a plus, but not always necessary. Parents need to feel comfortable with a babysitter. Sometimes just knowing the babysitter is enough. Even so, there are certain qualities that a babysitter should have:

- **Loves children**: A babysitter needs to love being around children. Children will be able to sense how you feel about them.

- **Responsible**: You are in charge of a child's well-being. Being dependable and mature are at the core of that task. Be knowledgeable about basic childcare duties such as feeding, dressing, bathing, and changing nappies.

- **Healthy**: If you are sick or have a contagious disease, avoid babysitting until you are well. You never know how it could affect a young child or infant.

- **Self-confident**: Be sure of yourself. Children will judge you on **instinct**. Project yourself as a strong person in order to gain their respect for your **authority**.

- **Respectful**: Be friendly and polite with the children and parents. Honour their privacy by not going through their personal possessions, cupboards, and drawers.

- **Safety-minded**: Be aware of what the children are doing at all times to keep them from harm. In an emergency be calm and collected.

How old is old enough to babysit?

Children mature at very different rates, so it is difficult to say that one age is old enough for all babysitters. It is up to the judgement of parents to decide if a babysitter seems old and mature enough to take on the job. It could be helpful to discuss with a parent or trusted adult whether or not you are mature and responsible enough to babysit. You can also look closely at yourself to decide if you are mature enough for the task.

Babysitting is more than just a job. You must possess a strong desire to care for children. Make sure you understand all the responsibilities of being a babysitter before you pursue becoming one.

↓

DID YOU KNOW?

Children who choose to do newspaper rounds or work in shops are covered by health and safety law but children who choose babysitting to earn money are not.

Both RoSPA and the NSPCC recommend that no one under 16 should be left alone to care for a baby. The British Red Cross say that children on their courses must be 14 by the time of their final assessment.

Do your research

Look at books on basic childcare in your local library. This will help teach you about issues you will encounter as a babysitter.

Try talking to family members and friends about their babysitting and childcare experiences. Maybe your parents can warn you about challenges you once posed to your babysitters! Other people's experience is always very valuable.

Babysitting younger family members is a great way to gain experience. At first, try babysitting with someone who has babysitting experience. Closely watch what they do and ask to help out as much as possible. They will be able to give you advice and tips. This will make you feel more confident when it is time to babysit on your own.

Courses and certification

Being a babysitter is a non-stop learning experience – every time you will notice or encounter something new. This on-the-job experience is the best kind, but it doesn't hurt to further your education outside the job. There are numerous different organisations that provide courses and **certification** for babysitting as well as related safety courses. Parents of the children you babysit will appreciate the responsibility displayed by taking a course. It will increase their confidence in you, which will put them at ease.

Getting it Right

Try looking into some of the following organisations. (Contact information is on page 53.)

- The British Red Cross provides various courses specialising in babysitting, first aid and other related safety courses.

- 4 Children is a national children's charity that provides support and information for all children and young people in their local community.

- RoSPA offers safety advice and education for young people and provides babysitting guidance.

- Online certification courses are available at websites such as Babysitting Class. Check with an adult before signing up.

- Many local colleges offer babysitting courses, safety courses, and **seminars** on related topics. Go online or check your local directories for listings and information.

Taking classes to properly educate yourself on child safety will make you a more valuable babysitter. This education will also provide you with the confidence needed in emergency situations.

FINDING WORK

After you have determined that you are qualified and you have done your homework, it is time to start looking for babysitting work. The following ideas might help you build up a **client** base:

- Ask your parents/guardians to give your name to their friends and colleagues at work.

- Inform your teachers or youth group leaders that you are a babysitter.

- Ask friends and other babysitters to give your name as a replacement if they cannot take on a job.

- Make a flyer or a simple business card to advertise your availability.

Babysitter for Hire

Name
Include a brief introduction of who you are and where you live (but not your specific address).

Contact information
List how and when to get in contact with you.

Pay rate
List what you charge for one child and how much more you will charge for each additional child.

Availability
List when you can or cannot babysit.

Training
List courses or classes you have taken related to babysitting.

Experience
Give details of how long you have been babysitting and what age groups you are comfortable with.

References
Ask that you be contacted to provide references. (To respect the referee's privacy, you should not list their contact information on the flyer.)

If you decide to make a flyer, it should have an eye-catching heading announcing that you are a "Babysitter for Hire." Include details such as on the example above.

Business cards

In addition to making a flyer, having a business card to hand out is a great idea as well. A business card is a small paper card about the size of credit card. It should have your name and contact information on it. There are many computer applications you can use to make these yourself, or check out some prices to have them professionally made by a printer.

Parents you currently babysit for will appreciate having a business card, as it will give them easy access to your contact information whenever they need it. It's also a convenient way to advertise your availability to potential new clients. People you give a business card to may not currently need your services, but if they ever did they would have your contact details to hand.

Keeping a diary

Using a diary to keep track of everything going on in your life is essential if you want to be a successful babysitter. Choose a small, notebook-style diary that is easy to carry around with you. It is most important that the diary you choose has enough space to write multiple entries per day, just in case you have several events going on. Try to write down anything that comes up immediately so you don't forget later. Having a diary handy will make it simple to schedule babysitting jobs around

Getting it Wrong

Don't just put up your flyer all over town or post it in letterboxes. Deliver it in person to **prospective** households. That way, they can meet you, plus you won't have complete strangers calling your home. You may want to avoid posting your flyer on the Internet for the same reason. However you decide to market yourself, always consult with a trusted adult to ensure your own safety comes first.

other important events in your life such as school, homework, sports, and having fun. Remember not to take on too many jobs at first and to schedule in some fun time, too!

TAKING ON A JOB

Before agreeing to take on a babysitting job, ask for references from the family and check up on them, especially if the family is unfamiliar. Sometimes it is easiest to work for families you know, perhaps friends of the family or neighbours, but this is not always possible.

Accepting a babysitting job means you are accepting the responsibility of caring for, and protecting, a child. Only accept a babysitting job if you are fully able to perform all the tasks that go with it.

Also make sure you are available. School projects, tests, and sporting events are all possible conflicts with babysitting. The easiest way to avoid conflicts is to keep track of your schedule by using a calendar or diary. You should also always double-check with your parents to get their approval before you agree to a job. Make sure you give your parents the contact details of the family you will be babysitting for.

• CHECKLIST •

The following are important questions to ask before taking on a babysitting job:

- How many hours will be required?
- Is the job daily or weekly?
- What time will the job finish?
- Will the job be during the week or on weekends?
- Will the parents take you home, especially at night?

Getting it Right

Only accept a babysitting job with which you are comfortable. Sometimes a job will be too long or there will be multiple children of different ages or with possible medical conditions. If the responsibility is too much, it is okay to say no. It is important to feel safe, too. If you are scared of your employer, the children, their house, or neighbourhood, it is best to decline the job politely. Be honest with yourself and others about what you can handle.

Living up to your commitment

Once you have lined up clients and babysitting jobs, you must remember that this is a serious commitment. Families are counting on you – this is a job that you must take very seriously. You should only back out if it is unavoidable or an emergency.

Once you agree to a job, you have entered into a **verbal contract**. It can hurt your **reputation** and babysitting business to back out at the last minute. But if you ever have to work when you would rather be somewhere else, do not show your disappointment at missing out on a fun event while you are babysitting. Always focus on being a normal, cheerful babysitter.

THE BUSINESS OF BABYSITTING

As enjoyable as babysitting can be, it is also a business that should be taken seriously. A babysitter provides a service and should expect a reasonable fee in return. Make a point to determine the pay rate before accepting the job. Doing this early will avoid any problems or awkwardness later.

The best way to come up with an initial pay rate is to ask friends or other babysitters what they are charging, or ask neighbours what they have paid in the past. That will give you a good idea of where to start.

Even babysitters need a business plan. Use your experience and training as a starting point for determining your pay rate. Ask other babysitters what they get paid, as well as what parents expect to pay in the area you will be babysitting in.

Q How experienced are you?

If you are young and new to babysitting, expect to be paid on the low end of what you have determined to be the average rate. If you have several years of experience, then be confident enough to raise your rate.

Q Where do you live?

If a babysitting job is far from where you live or is in an undesirable area, adjust your rate accordingly and reconsider whether or not the job is worth it.

Q What will your responsibilities be?

Find out immediately what is expected of you and if it involves more than keeping the children safe and entertained. Feel free to charge more, especially if you are expected to cook and clean.

Q What training do you have?

If you have completed any safety courses or received any babysitting training or certification, these are bonus qualities that most parents would be happy to pay a little extra for.

Q How many children will you be watching?

If there is more than one child, it is appropriate to charge a little extra, since the responsibility level increases.

Getting it Right

Bringing up the topic of money can be hard. It is best to do it up front by saying, "I normally charge _____," or, "The pay rate for this area is _____." You may find it helpful to practise this discussion about money ahead of time with someone you trust, such as a friend, teacher, or parent.

Don't sell yourself too short. The service of babysitting is very important, and people will respect that. Consider all factors when deciding a pay rate.

Q Is the fee hourly or by-the-job?

Most babysitters request an hourly pay rate so there is no confusion. But if you are always working similar hours with similar responsibilities, a "by-the-job" rate may be easier. Work it out with your employer ahead of time.

Q How old are you?

In most cases, the older you are the better. This is because parents will judge the maturity of babysitters based on their age.

Arrive and Prepare

The first time you meet potential new clients, remember to be very professional. This is an important opportunity so be sure to treat it like one.

FIRST IMPRESSIONS

First **impressions** are important when meeting someone for the first time. With babysitting, a good first impression is very important if you expect to be asked back or given a good referral. Sometimes the first time you meet a family will be when you arrive at a new job. So make your impression count.

Getting to know the children

Remember that the children might be frightened at first. Children can be very attached to their parents, so they might feel a lot of anxiety over the fact that their parents will soon be leaving them with a stranger. Don't take it personally if the children do not seem to want to get to know you at first – this is normal.

Do everything you can to make the children feel at ease. Kneel down to introduce yourself to each child at his or her eye level. Let the children get used to you before getting close or picking them up. Call them by their names and ask them questions – for example, ask them about a toy they are playing with or a pet that is nearby.

If you show interest in the children and you seem warm and caring, this will help them to relax around you. The job of being a babysitter is a lot easier if the children like you. Take the time to get to know them.

← *A parent should be put at ease with how babysitters present themselves. Act like a professional when reporting to a job, and always make a good first impression.*

TIP

Do not let your standards slip. Whether you are babysitting for a new family, or some of your own family members or friends you know well, you should remain professional at all times.

GET TO KNOW THE FAMILY ROUTINES

Before the parents leave, it is worth asking them for any special instructions or whether the children have any specific needs you should consider or cater for.

Household rules and handling misbehaviour

Inquire about how the parents would like you to handle their children's behaviour. Find out exactly what the children are allowed and not allowed to do. Discuss appropriate consequences like no TV or being sent to their rooms.

Homework and chores

Ask if homework and chores should be completed before the children are allowed to watch TV, eat snacks, or play with toys or friends.

Medication

Discuss medical conditions. You should not be expected to give, or take responsibility for, any child's medicine. If medication needs to be given to children, the parents should take responsibility for this.

Food

What food should the children have, and at what time should they eat? Are there any foods they are **allergic** to or cannot eat? What are their likes and dislikes?

TIP

Don't forget to ask the children some questions before the parents leave. Ask how they are. Do they have any ideas for what they want to do while you are there? As the parents will still be around, consult them if the children say something is wrong or request something you aren't sure is allowed.

Playtime

Determine where the children are allowed to play – inside or outside.

Pets

If there are pets, ask if you need to feed them or give them water. Ask how you are to care for the animals.

Friends

Are the children allowed to have friends over? If so, you need contact details of the friend's parents.

Bath and bed

Ask what time the children should be in bed and if they need to take a bath beforehand. Make sure it is okay with the parents that you help the children in the bath.

Cleaning

Locate all the cleaning supplies that you might need to tidy up. If nappies are involved, find out where the parents would like you to change and dispose of the nappies.

Spend some time discussing with the parents everything that is expected of you while you are babysitting. Write down all rules and important information so it is not forgotten.

IMPORTANT INFORMATION

Find out where the parents are going. If it is a restaurant, get the name, address, and phone number. Get their mobile phone number too. If they are going from place to place, like dinner and then to the cinema, get all the relevant addresses and phone numbers. Also find out when they expect to be arriving at and leaving each place. Ask what time they will be home and if they are expecting any phone calls or visitors, and how you should handle either if they occur. Write down all messages with details that are easy to understand.

It might sound like you are asking for too much information, but if something goes wrong, you want to be able to find the parents immediately.

TIP

Get more than just a mobile number from parents – mobiles can get lost or have a bad signal.

Make a list of all the contact information provided by the parents. Include all local emergency phone numbers. Keep this list on you, or in a place that is easy to find – like near the phone or on the fridge.

→

Emergency contact list

Ask the parents for a specific contact list of whom to contact first in an emergency if they cannot be reached. Get trusted friends and neighbours' numbers, as well as local emergency numbers for fire, police, and the hospital or doctor. Write down the address of the house you are babysitting at in case it is needed in an emergency.

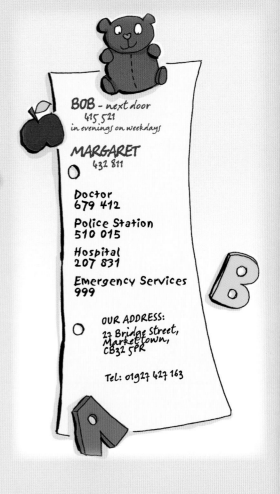

BOB – next door
415 521
in evenings on weekdays

MARGARET
432 811

Doctor
679 412

Police Station
510 015

Hospital
207 831

Emergency Services
999

OUR ADDRESS:
23 Bridge Street,
Market Town,
CB32 5PR

Tel: 01927 427 163

Know your surroundings

All homes and neighbourhoods are different. Get comfortable with both. Make certain you know the safe road crossings near the house. Enquire about the local area and if there are places to avoid.

Take a tour of the house with the parents. Ask them to show you what doors and windows need to be locked, and if there are any keys you should have.

Make sure all fire alarms work. Find out if there is a fire escape or **evacuation** plan for a fire or other natural disaster. If not, come up with one yourself and practise it with the children. Ask if there are any known existing **hazards** and inspect the house for any potential ones.

Getting it Right

- Have a fire evacuation plan.
- If there is a fire, don't hide and remain calm.
- Avoid smoke by staying low to the ground.
- Feel doors and doorknobs for heat. If they are hot, fire is behind them – do not open them.
- Stop, drop, and roll on the ground if you catch on fire.
- Once outside a burning house, do not return inside.

Find out where all fire escapes and emergency exits are in the building. Knowing how to escape in an emergency saves valuable time and could save your life, and the lives of those in your care.

Embrace the household's culture

Every family is different. They may have different rules, traditions, backgrounds, and beliefs than your own. Respect their differences. A babysitter should take the time to understand the basic culture and religion of families who are regular clients.

Talk to the parents about any religious food restrictions. Find out if there are any special practices or prayers you might have to help the children do or say. Certain words or entertainment like television may be offensive to their heritage. Ask to be sure.

Be sensitive to their background. Consider researching the heritage of the children to be able to understand their culture, so that you can communicate with them about it. You can talk about your background, but it is not your place to push your beliefs or to comment on theirs.

You are expected to make the children comfortable – that's what you are there for. Accept the differences and try to blend in, but if you are uncomfortable with the family's lifestyle or beliefs, you may need to refuse to take on the job.

Cover yourself

Keeping the children you are babysitting safe should be your first priority, but don't forget about yourself. Alert your parents, relatives, and friends to where you will be babysitting and how to reach you in an emergency. Explain to them how long you will be working, what sort of **itinerary** you have planned, and whether or not you need transportation.

Arrange pick-up and check-in times, especially if this is a new job. Always trust your instincts and feelings. If something doesn't feel right, or a parent of the children you are babysitting for acts inappropriately, tell someone you trust immediately.

Each household is different, and a family's backgrounds and traditions could be very different from your own. Learning about a family's heritage is beneficial as it will make both you and the family you are working for more comfortable.

NEED TO KNOW

1) When do you give a child medicine?
a) Whenever a child feels sick.
b) Every four to six hours.
c) Never.

2) What should you make sure you ask the parents before they leave?
a) What their favourite food is.
b) The vital information about where they are going.
c) The names of their pets.

3) How do you know who to call first in an emergency?
a) Ask a child you are babysitting.
b) Set up an emergency call list ahead of time.
c) Look on the Internet.

4) What information about the house should you be aware of?
a) The location of first aid and medical supplies.
b) If the basement floods.
c) The age of the house.

5) How should you keep yourself safe?
a) Hire a body guard.
b) Take karate lessons.
c) Tell friends and relatives where and when you are babysitting.

6) What should you do if a parent acts inappropriately towards you?
a) Call the police.
b) Ignore it.
c) Tell someone you trust.

Check the answers on page 50 to see if you know it all.

SAFETY AND CARE

The primary duty of a babysitter is to keep children safe. Keep safety in mind at all times. Don't just think safe – prepare to be safe as well. Anything can happen at any time, so be ready.

FIRST THINGS FIRST

After the parents leave, make sure the house is secure. Lock windows and doors. Don't answer the door to strangers, and don't tell anyone who calls that you are alone with children. Screen calls with the answering machine.

Avoid getting distracted. Even losing focus for a few minutes can give children enough time to get into trouble. Don't use the phone or computer unless you absolutely must.

Keep your focus on the children

Focus on the children at all times. Keep the children in your sight. It doesn't take long for children to get in trouble, so stay close. Involve yourself in whatever they are doing so that you can stay alert. After a short amount of time with a child, you will begin to recognise certain tendencies. For instance, if you know the child likes to explore, then stay a step ahead.

Making your environment safe

Safety comes first when caring for children so keep these things in mind.

Inside

- Ensure the parents have placed any medicines, cleaning supplies or similar items, which may contain harmful chemicals, somewhere the children cannot reach them.

- Be aware of hazards like uncovered electrical outlets, tools, and other sharp objects, as well as potentially dangerous areas like stairs.

- Keep the children away from any small objects that can be swallowed such as coins, pins, or small toys. Dispose of, or move, plastic bags and other items that can **suffocate**.

- Check all toys for hazards like strings that can choke, and make sure they are appropriate for whatever age the child is. An older child's toy, such as a kite, could be very dangerous to younger children if they get tangled in the string.

Outside

- Keep children away from the street. Lock gates or doors that can lead to streets, pools, patios, porches, balconies, or other dangerous areas. Never leave children alone on an outdoor area like a balcony, especially if it is above ground and they can fall.

- Keep young children away from moving objects like swings, bikes, and cars. If they are old enough to use a swing or other playground equipment, check to make sure the equipment is safe.

- Establish a firm set of outdoor rules before the children are allowed to play.

Getting it Right

You are there to babysit and nothing else. Don't talk on the phone unless you have to, and never use the Internet unless you have been given permission. Even if the parents do give permission, it is not a good idea, as it is a distraction from your job of watching the children. Also, if you damage the computer or visit a questionable website, it could hurt your chances of future jobs.

FIRST AID

Always locate a **sterile** first aid kit in the home where you are babysitting. Hopefully you will not have to use it. Minor bruises, cuts, nosebleeds, and non-severe burns can be easy to deal with but remember: you are not a doctor.

If a child gets injured, do not panic. Call the parents, or someone from your emergency telephone number list, immediately. If the injury is severe, where there is a lot of bleeding and pain, or it appears to be life-threatening, call the police or another emergency rescue number from your prepared phone list. The most important thing you can do in an emergency is keep calm.

A first aid kit is essential to any babysitting job. Make certain you know where one is located in each household you are babysitting for. It's not a bad idea to carry one with you wherever you work, just in case a family does not have an adequate one.

Life-saving techniques

Learning life-saving techniques like **CPR** and the **Heimlich manoeuvre** might be something you want to consider doing to give you confidence in an emergency. Local hospitals, colleges, and the Red Cross (see page 53 for contact details) often hold classes, but it is worth bearing in mind that some may have age restrictions.

TIP

To avoid choking hazards, do not give children food like popcorn or small sweets that they can choke on, and cut their food into bite-sized pieces. Keep any objects they could choke on out of reach.

Water safety

Give children a bath only if a parent asks you to do so. If giving a young child a bath is part of the job, be very careful. Test the water to make sure it is warm, but not too hot. Never leave a young child alone in the bathroom, especially in the bath. If the phone rings, ignore it and let the answering machine take a message. Water can be one of the greatest dangers you will face as a babysitter. Whether it is a bathtub or a pool, children can drown in only a couple inches of water and not even make a sound, so you must stay with them at all times.

CPR

CPR is an emergency procedure that gets the breathing and blood circulation going. This could be especially important in an emergency situation involving water and drowning.

Heimlich manoeuvre

The Heimlich manoeuvre is a procedure that helps dislodge something on which a person is choking. With infants and children, this could be important if they choke on food or manage to swallow something they shouldn't.

Getting it Right

If there is a swimming pool, you might want to tell the parents you would rather the children did not swim. This is completely acceptable, and the parents will appreciate that you show this level of concern.

QUIZ

SAFETY SENSE

1) What is the primary duty of a babysitter?
a) To have good, clean fun with children.
b) To keep children safe.
c) To teach children how to cook.

2) When should you talk on the phone?
a) If your best friend calls.
b) If the children want to.
c) If it is absolutely necessary.

3) How often should you use the computer or Internet?
a) Only if you are given permission.
b) Whenever you want.
c) If a child asks you.

4) What should you never do when bathing young children?
a) Leave them alone in the bathroom.
b) Use a washcloth.
c) Sing them songs.

5) Why take a safety course?
a) To make you a more complete babysitter.
b) So you are more confident in an emergency.
c) All of the above.

Check the answers on page 50 to see how much safety sense you have.

28

Taking Control

Children are not going to be pleasant 100 percent of the time. They will have their good moods and bad moods, just like anyone else. Not surprisingly, children will even misbehave. It's okay – that is all just part of growing up. A lot of the time it is not even their fault. Don't think they're bad children because of it.

Recognising misbehaviour

Misbehaviour or any form of acting up can be related to the child's environment or the people around them. If children are uncomfortable or even too comfortable, they can act up. A child could be in a room with few or no toys and misbehave out of boredom. The same child could be in a room with lots of toys and become so excited that misbehaviour begins. Misbehaviour is often a cry for attention that usually means something caused the child to be uncomfortable or **overstimulated**.

DID YOU KNOW?

Children often misbehave when they feel the following ways:
- Tired
- Sick
- Hungry/thirsty
- Bored
- Overstimulated/excited
- Upset
- Scared
- In need of attention.

When children misbehave, there is always a reason but finding what that reason is can be puzzling. As a babysitter you need to identify what a child needs to stop bad behaviour. Always talk with a child to find out exactly what it is they want, so you can respond properly. Siblings can often help a babysitter work this out.

PREVENTING MISBEHAVIOUR

Preventing misbehaviour before it occurs is the best strategy. Take time to surround children with a happy, positive environment and structure the time you spend with them with routines they recognise. This will keep the children in line and make the job more enjoyable for you.

Stay positive

Use encouraging words with children. If they are behaving well, let them know. They will enjoy the attention and recognise good behaviour as a way to be noticed. Go with the flow while babysitting. It is important not to be stressed or upset. You want to create a welcoming environment for the children. If a child does something wrong, like spills something, check they are not injured and calmly clean it up. Don't get angry – it's no big deal.

Explain limits

Tell children exactly how you expect them to act in each situation or environment you encounter with them. Limits such as, "You can roll the ball in the kitchen, but do not throw it", allow children to know what is expected of them. Don't overwhelm children with too many rules – instead set clear limits they can understand.

Let them choose

Children feel good if they are allowed to make a decision. It can give them a sense of **empowerment** that is good for self-confidence. Allowing them to make controlled choices with food and entertainment will keep them happy, which will keep you happy.

Humour them

Humour can win over a child if used effectively. All young children love to laugh, so it is generally an easy task to make them do so. Using humour can remove tension from a situation to prevent conflict – for example, "I see a lot of frowning faces in here, we can't play outside unless we all start smiling."

Give warnings

Always let children know if they are getting out of control. Calmly explain what will happen if they don't behave. Let children know in advance what is going to happen – for example, "Five more minutes until bed time, so start clearing up."

Plan ahead

If you already know certain situations and environments cause misbehaviour, be sure to avoid them. Bring toys or games and plan activities to keep the children occupied.

Set an example

Act how you want the children to act. If you expect children to clean up after themselves, be sure to clean up after yourself. Children will always look up to you. Use that as an advantage.

DEALING WITH BAD BEHAVIOUR

If you were not able to prevent bad behaviour, don't worry. You can deal with bad behaviour already in progress with the following strategies.

Distraction

The attention span of a young child is short. If children are doing something you disapprove of, **coax** them into another direction. Either change the toy they are playing with or move them away from a situation.

Calm them down

Take them to one side and calmly talk them into settling down.

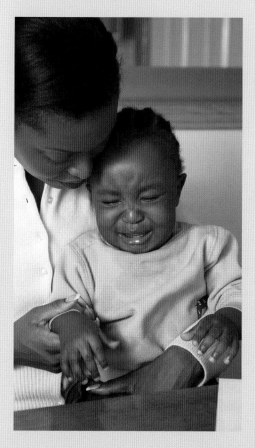

Ignore them

Most misbehaviour revolves around getting attention. Try ignoring children who misbehave in order to get your attention, but stay alert to what they are doing and if they are safe. Only give them attention if they behave – for example, say, "I can only see good little boys and girls today. Bad ones are invisible."

Suggest different behaviour

Simply ask misbehaving children to do something else. If they are running in the house, ask them to walk in slow motion like they are on the moon. Hopefully they will think it's fun.

Teach consequences

Children learn from the consequences of their actions. If children are mean and no one plays with them, they will learn to be nice very quickly. Helping them learn these lessons is better than **reprimanding** them or yelling.

Babysitting isn't always fun and games. From time to time a child will become upset. Be encouraging and comforting to a distressed child.

31

STAGES OF DEVELOPMENT

Understanding how children are behaving is easier if you have a good grasp of their stages of development. Children have different needs, depending on their age and maturity level.

Always try to be aware of the particular characteristics of each child you are babysitting. Understanding a child's level of development will help you make better choices, which makes your job easier.

Children of different ages will be at different levels of development. Understand that what is easy for one child could be difficult for another. Use different activities for different aged children or find something that everyone can do.

6–12 months	1–3 years	3–5 years	5+ years
Infants	**Toddlers**	**Young children**	**Older children**

6–12 months — Infants

- Nap in the morning and afternoon.
- Have set eating and sleeping times.
- Begin trying to feed themselves, but still need help.
- Crawl around.
- Can pick up and throw objects.
- Are sometimes able to walk with hand-holding help.
- Respond to their name.
- Fear new people and being left alone.
- Become upset when they want something.
- Start learning what they can and cannot do.
- Make babbling sounds.

1–3 years — Toddlers

- Can feed themselves for the most part, but are often sloppy.
- Are possessive of objects they feel should be theirs, and want to do things by themselves.
- Are emotional, with frequent temper tantrums.
- Feel secure when they are aware that parents are around.
- Want to be the centre of attention.
- Do not like to share.
- Enjoy exploring their surroundings.
- Like playing by themselves.
- Begin to speak and often say, "No," "Me," and "Mine."

3–5 years — Young children

- Have more strength, control, and balance with their bodies.
- Enjoy physical activities and challenges like running and dancing.
- Can draw, paint, and are learning to write.
- Begin playing with other children, but prefer to be around the same sex.
- Often tell on each other for attention.
- Enjoy helping adults with chores, also for attention.
- Understand what is right, wrong, and expected of them.
- Able to express themselves and communicate.
- Enjoy humour and being silly.
- Don't like being criticised or ignored.

5+ years — Older children

- Are energetic and active.
- Are self-conscious and seek acceptance.
- Show independence, which will sometimes include disobedience and talking back.
- Like to share ideas and thoughts.
- Experience friendship and look up to older children.
- Have changing interests and the desire to try new things.

DISCIPLINE

If you are spending a lot of time babysitting for the same family, the parents may feel it is necessary to set up certain guidelines for their children's misbehaviour. Parents will usually feel very strongly about how their children are disciplined, if at all. It is best to check with them first about how and for what the children should be disciplined. You might also find it helpful to offer rewards and **incentives** for good behaviour.

Getting it Right

Parents may want you to leave the disciplining to them. A "time out" can be an effective alternative.

- Remove children from a misbehaving situation to let them know what they are doing is wrong.

- Use a clock or kitchen timer to let children know how long they will have a "time out." It doesn't have to be long. A couple of minutes are an eternity to a child.

- It won't be long before children learn that behaving is a whole lot more fun than misbehaving and needing to have a time out.

- Congratulate children on completing the time out and encourage them not to need a time out again – say, for example, "It's no fun for your babysitter when you have a time out, either."

Infants

Do not discipline infants. With infants, as well as with all children you are babysitting, no hitting, spanking, slapping, shaking, or shouting is ever appropriate. Infants cannot understand what you are saying, so it is pointless to shout at them.

If infants cry and will not stop, it is not because they are misbehaving. Infants cannot talk, so they cry to communicate. Infants grow and learn every day. The first thing they learn is to cry. They cry if they want something, are sick, or are hurt.

A babysitter needs to do a little detective work to figure out what is wrong with infants. If infants continue to cry, keep trying every calming technique you can. Try holding and slightly rocking them. Sometimes infants will cry until they are exhausted and fall asleep. If all else fails, don't be afraid to call the parents for guidance. That will show responsibility and caring, which the parents will appreciate.

Toddlers and older children

If rules and guidelines are already in place, toddlers and especially older children will know how to behave. Again, check with parents on how to handle various disciplinary situations. Toddlers at least need to be told in a calm manner that what they are doing is wrong, especially when safety is a concern.

Certain actions or situations may call for discipline. For example, if children wander out of view repeatedly or fool around in areas with cleaning supplies or other hazardous materials, this is a safety issue that needs to be responded to. Biting, hitting, and other fighting are safety issues that require a calm response from the babysitter.

Finally, disobeying repeated instructions or directions (for instance, throwing toys after being told not to), being **possessive** and not sharing, speaking rudely, talking back, or using **profanity** are all actions that require some discipline.

It is important to maintain the same level of discipline for each offence. One child should not get away with misbehaving if another has already been punished. If two children are fighting, they should be given equal "time out" periods, regardless of who started it.

ENFORCING ROUTINES

It is important for babysitters to follow the routines of children's lives. But when children are under the care of a babysitter, they can sometimes resist following these routines.

You will find it helpful to learn the mealtime routines for the children you are babysitting. A child will probably need to eat at some point, so it is good to know ahead of time what they enjoy or should eat. This could help prevent any feeding difficulties.

Mealtime

Mealtime routines can quickly feel out of control for a babysitter. Children are often picky eaters, or younger children can play with or throw their food and utensils. As previously mentioned, it helps if you have already established all the routines of mealtime with the parents – for example, know what the children's favourite foods are and what time they usually eat their meals. Beyond this, do the best you can if the children refuse to eat.

It is not possible to force children to eat, and the more frustrated and anxious you get about it, the more anxious they will feel. Sometimes it works to take a break and try again later. For younger children, also try games, such as making a spoon a "plane" that flies into the child's mouth.

Do the best you can to get the children to finish their food, but understand that mealtimes are often difficult. If the children do not eat well, make sure you mention this to the parents after they return.

Getting it Right

You can structure your time with older children around homework. Use this as a way to control the environment by presenting homework as a task the children have to achieve before they can play or watch TV. Parents will be impressed and extremely thankful, since it will be one less thing they will have to do. They might even give you a payrise!

TIP

Sometimes children won't eat just because the parents aren't around. It is okay if they don't want to eat because they feel sick or just are not hungry. But it can help to encourage them to eat their meal by promising a reward if they do. Offer them a dessert or special treat if they finish their meal. Or suggest a fun game to play if they eat all their food. You can even tell them they can choose the fun activity!

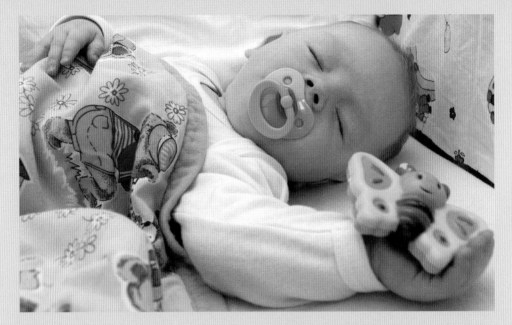

Time for bed

Putting children to bed is not as easy as simply tucking them in. Talk to the parents about each child's bedtime routine. Try to follow the routine as closely as possible to make the children comfortable enough to fall asleep normally. You often need to calm children down to get them to sleep.

Getting a child to go to sleep can be tricky. But what's most important is that they are comfortable. Make sure their sleeping environment is peaceful and surrounded with items that make them feel content.

Reading a story or playing soft music can relax them. Infants can be a little more challenging. Softly singing or playing calming music while lightly holding or rocking them can help. Don't be surprised if putting an infant to sleep takes a while.

Be alert and available if any children wake. All children have the potential to be in danger if they wake up and try to move around in the dark.

Check on sleeping children frequently. Be ready for nightmares, children needing a drink, or any other "can't sleep" events. When putting them back to bed, speak softly and calmly to coax them back to sleep.

TIP

Can't get the children to sleep? Offer "rewards for next time", like treats or special privileges as an incentive for staying in bed and going to sleep.

QUIZ

WELL BEHAVED

1) How do you stop a child from misbehaving?
a) Shout and scream at the child.
b) Identify what the child needs.
c) Call the parents.

2) How can you prevent cases of misbehaviour?
a) Know the causes of misbehaviour.
b) Act tough and mean.
c) Promise treats for good behaviour.

3) What can often be the cause of misbehaviour? Being:
a) tired.
b) sick.
c) hungry.
d) all of the above.

4) What is the strategy for preventing misbehaviour?
a) Explain clear and easy limits and rules ahead of time.
b) Send children to their rooms.
c) Scare them with stories of monsters that kidnap bad children.

5) What is an easy way to deal with misbehaviour?
a) Threaten the children.
b) Pretend it's not happening.
c) Calmly talk them into settling down.

6) Why is it good to let a child make some decisions?
a) They know more about their surroundings than you.
b) It will give them self confidence.
c) You have too much to worry about as it is.

7) Why should sleeping children be checked on frequently?
a) To practise spying on them.
b) To stop the bed bugs from biting.
c) To make sure they aren't in any danger.

Check the answers on page 50 to see how much you have learned about behaviour and routines.

Have Some Fun

When it comes down to it, children of all ages just want to have fun. Don't be afraid to have some fun yourself. Watching TV is fine for a little bit, but you will never get to know the children properly if the TV is distracting everyone.

GET INTERACTIVE

Switch off the TV and start playing with the children. Find whatever their favourite toy is at the moment and tempt them over with it. If they are older kids, ask them questions about it to get them going.

Children love to have fun while being active. Activities can be fun, educational, and extremely beneficial to a child's development. Games help children form social skills, gain confidence, and practise communication.

Ice breakers

The children you are babysitting should be excited when they see you. Even if you are meeting the children for the first time, try to impress them right away with fun and excitement. Start off your time with them with a game. A quick game of tag, hide and seek, or even some light wrestling around are good ways to get children to open up to you and have fun.

TIP

Come prepared. Make up a "babysitting survival kit" to take with you on each job. Stock it with playing cards, board games, storybooks, art materials, and even simple costumes. This way, if the children get bored with their normal play routines, you can introduce a fresh, new idea to captivate them.

Playing games and other activities are a great way to get to know children while having fun. Puzzles are an easy activity that is both fun and skill-building for a child.

→

DIFFERENT AGES OF FUN

Children are different in size, age, and maturity. So, that means you will have to be ready with different kinds of fun. It shouldn't be that difficult to think of some fun ideas. If you are having trouble, just try to imagine what you thought was fun as a child. Or, better still, ask them what they think is fun. Do your best to ensure that the children have a good time. You will enjoy the experience, and the children will ask their parents if you can babysit again.

Infants

Entertaining very young children is not difficult. Do simple things to amuse them, like softly reading or singing. Try playing pat-a-cake or games similar to "peek-a-boo," where you hide your face with your hands or a pillow and then reveal it.

Infants have a good time just crawling around. Put them on a blanket or towel and drag them around a little bit. Don't get too wild – just tug them a short way here and there. Make sure you are in a safe area.

Toddlers

Toddlers like exploring just about anything. Put their curious hands to work. Give them building blocks or even plastic food storage containers and get them to stack them up and knock them down. They will be thrilled to see their towers crumble to the ground. As long as the objects used are safe, everyone has fun.

Picture books are also great for toddlers. Anything with animals will be good for them to leaf through and point at. Encourage them to mimic the sounds different animals make.

Getting it Right

Utilise children's creative energy – and then prepare yourself for a wild ride! Children enjoy trying to create or build just about anything. Build a fort with them in the living room out of pillows and blankets. Let them paint or colour in colouring books at the kitchen table. Another option is sculpting with clay and constructing easy craft projects. Who knows – maybe you will inspire them to be an artist someday.

Children are at their happiest when they are having fun. An easy way to get them to have fun is to get them moving. Get them dancing by adding a little music to their environment or inspire them to act out fantasy scenarios, like a mini play.

Older children

Children who can walk and talk are at a stage where activities need to have a little more entertainment value. These children enjoy playing "pretend" games. Make up a story that you all play out. You could have everyone pretend the house is a castle, and assign each child a different title of royalty like "prince" or "princess." Dress everyone up in costumes if you can, even if it is just using bath towels as capes. Then play it out and see where their imaginations take you.

Try playing cards, a board game, or working on a puzzle together. Get them talking by asking them questions about the activity you are doing. You'll be surprised at the answers and funny stories that they come up with. Children like feeling that they are "big kids," too. This is a great way to bond with them.

FUN IN MOTION

As long as it is safe and okay with the parents, get the children moving. Exercise is good for growing children, so parents might appreciate it if you gave their kids a little workout.

- Introduce them to sports by playing catch or just kicking a ball around. (You should only do this outdoors.)

- Set up a scavenger hunt in which the children have to find various objects around the house.

- Take them on field trips, even if it is just around the house. Pretend you are in a jungle and are searching for exotic animals.

- Put on some music and have a dance party. Children love jumping around. But be careful not to let the dancing get too wild.

- Cook with them. Check with the parents first about what foods are okay and if there are special instructions for feeding infants. Again, keep it simple. Avoid actually cooking with heat or using knives with the children. You want the children to participate and feel like they are helping, but your first concern should be that they are safe.

FUN . . . WITHOUT TV?

It is possible to have fun without watching TV or a film. Use your imagination, and ask other people for ideas. A lot of times children will be able to come up with something on their own. Listen to them, and go with their ideas even if they are silly. The silliest ideas are often the most fun!

Board games

Try fun, easy games that don't take hours to play or have many rules to learn.

Play "I Spy"

Describe objects until the children can work out what you are describing – for example, "I Spy, with my little eye, something yellow that you peel and eat." If they guess right – in this case, a banana – let them have a turn.

Fashion show

Get everyone to put on outfits and strut down the hallway like a catwalk.

Some children may be too young to participate in every activity. A quick game of "peek-a-boo" can include even the youngest children in on the fun.

Piggyback rides and playing "aeroplane" or "train"

If you are comfortable and strong enough to pick up children, you can play make-believe for any scenario once they are in your arms. Carry them around while making up a story about a plane flight or train ride. Make announcements that you are the pilot or conductor. Make crash landings and emergency stops on soft couches and beds.

Game show trivia

Have contests where you ask the children various questions about topics they would know about. Use characters from stories and fairytales as answers or ask them about their family, pet, or house.

New hairstyle or makeovers

Experiment with wild hairstyles and makeup – but nothing permanent. Be sure to wash away any mess you make, especially on the child!

Telephone

Use a toy or disconnected phone and have children act out various imitations of people on the phone, such as a police officer, or Grandma.

Mirror images

Make different faces in the bathroom mirror. Hold contests for the wildest, funniest, scariest, and weirdest face!

Pretend performances

Pretend you are all famous characters, and get everyone to do quick performances of scenes they know from films or plays – or just make scenes up.

Seasonal crafts

Make festive decorations out of pinecones or branches and ribbon. You can also make greeting cards out of construction paper and decorate them with crayon or marker drawings.

Ancient toys

Gather up some of their toys and pretend each toy is an ancient object or treasure. These can be hidden around the house or in a fort to be "discovered." Later you can have a mock auction or museum display of all the artefacts.

Name that tune

Sing or hum songs the children would know and ask them to try to identify them. If they can't remember the name, have them at least say where they know the songs from.

Aerobics

Teach them basic exercises like jumping jacks, sit-ups, stretching, and running in place. Maybe find an old workout tape or DVD and try to imitate it with the children, being as silly as possible.

Guess that beast

Get everyone to take turns acting out an animal while everyone else guesses what it is.

Cardboard kingdom

Use old cardboard boxes to create imaginary settings like spaceships or pirate ships.

Pavement chalk

If the children are allowed outside while you babysit, draw chalk pictures on the pavement or driveway. Try drawing portraits of each other.

Magazine art

Take some old magazines and cut out people, animals, cars, homes, buildings, and plants. Have the children tape or paste them together to create different scenes. These could be presents for the parents when they get home.

FINISH UP

Tidy up the house before the parents return. Even if they tell you cleaning is not part of the job, you should still make an effort to pick up any loose items that could easily be put away. At least leave the house exactly as it was when you started the job. Clean up any messes you made and try to return the children in the same clean condition as well!

Getting it Right

Give the parents a full report of all the activities you did and whether or not anything noteworthy happened. Make sure to give them any messages if anyone called.

Always clean up after yourself. You shouldn't feel like you have to clean the entire house, but you should make sure any mess you or the children made while you were there is cleaned up before the parents come home.

THAT'S ENTERTAINMENT

1) **What can you do to get a child to interact with you?**
   a) Ask them questions.
   b) Turn on the TV.
   c) Talk on the phone.

2) **Why are playful games beneficial to a child's development? They:**
   a) aid in learning how to sit still and be quiet.
   b) teach them how to survive in the wild.
   c) help them form social skills.

3) **What is a good ice breaker game to play with children?**
   a) Cooking in the kitchen.
   b) Hide and seek.
   c) Room cleaning.

4) **How can you entertain very young children?**
   a) Quiz them with simple maths problems.
   b) Softly read or sing to them.
   c) Ask them questions about current events.

5) **What are some good ways to have fun while exercising?**
   a) Playing sports.
   b) Having a dance party.
   c) All of the above.

6) **How should you leave the house when you've finished babysitting?**
   a) Exactly how you found it.
   b) A little bit messy to show you were doing something.
   c) Rearrange all furniture to the best of your ability.

Check the answers on page 50 to see how entertaining you can be!

To Sum It Up

Babysitting is a job for someone who is caring and responsible. Parents will not want to trust their children with just anyone, so it is important to demonstrate that you are qualified. Taking classes and courses related to babysitting will help show that even if you do not have a lot of experience, you still have the drive to learn and succeed.

PARENTAL PLEASERS

Above all, parents need to feel comfortable with you caring for their children. If you can put their minds at ease with how you present yourself, sometimes that is the only qualification needed. If you truly care about children, your enthusiasm for babysitting will definitely be noticed.

A good babysitter will have good social skills. Communicating with the parents is just as important as communicating with the children. Everyone involved needs to be on the same wavelength, to ensure that the experience is positive for the children. Be prepared to ask the parents anything that will benefit your caring for their children. A child's well-being is very important, so don't be shy. Parents will be very appreciative and willing to answer anything.

Play safely

Children's safety is the primary focus of a babysitter. You are expected to entertain the children, but always think about keeping them out of harm's way. Have fun, but don't take any risks, either. The activities you choose for them should reflect what their own parents would choose for them.

Attractive ambition

Babysitting is attractive to those interested in gaining not only job experience, but life experience, too. A job like babysitting shows **ambition** and maturity, which are two very impressive traits. One day you may pursue a career in childcare or have children yourself. It is important to develop these fundamental experiences, as they will benefit you in anything you do, from other jobs to relationships.

Happy children, happy parents, happy you!

Becoming a babysitter will help you learn about children and yourself. You will be faced with numerous choices and problems to which you must react. Approach each one with

48

patience. Have confidence in your decisions, as long as they are in the children's best interest.

Most children will sometimes misbehave or become upset. Be calm and encouraging when you talk to them. Make sure they understand the rules and respect that you are in charge. Remember, you are not there to mould the children – you are there to take care of them. Keep them safe and in good spirits. Happy children will make happy parents – which will result in a very happy, successful babysitter.

Before leaving, make sure you give the parents a full report on everything that happened while you were working. Make as good an impression leaving as you did when you arrived.

QUIZ RESULTS

NEED TO KNOW
For page 23

1) c) Never.

2) b) The vital information about where they are going.

3) b) Set up an emergency call list ahead of time.

4) a) The location of first aid and medical supplies.

5) c) Alert friends and relatives where and when you are babysitting.

6) c) Tell someone you trust.

WELL BEHAVED
For page 39

1) b) Identify what the child needs.

2) a) Know the causes of misbehaviour.

3) d) All of the above.

4) a) Explain clear and easy limits and rules ahead of time.

5) c) Calmly talk them into settling down.

6) b) It will give them self confidence.

7) c) To make sure they aren't in any danger.

SAFETY SENSE
For page 28

1) b) To keep children safe.

2) c) If it is absolutely necessary.

3) a) Only if you are given permission.

4) a) Leave them alone in the bathroom.

5) c) All of the above.

THAT'S ENTERTAINMENT
For page 47

1) a) Ask them questions.

2) c) Help them form social skills.

3) b) Hide and seek.

4) b) Softly reading or singing to them.

5) d) All of the above.

6) a) Exactly how you found it.

⬤20 Things To Remember

1 Make parents comfortable with you as their babysitter by showing qualities such as loving children and being responsible, healthy, self-confident, respectful, and safety-minded.

2 Before agreeing to a babysitting job, ask for references from the family and check up on them, especially if you are unfamiliar with the family.

3 Only accept a babysitting job you are comfortable with. Politely decline if you feel you cannot do the job for any reason.

4 Make a point to determine the pay rate before accepting a babysitting job.

5 A good first impression is very important if you expect to be asked back or be given a good referral.

6 Take the time to get to know the children you are babysitting – this will make everyone more comfortable.

7 Before the parents leave, ask for any special instructions or if the children have any special needs.

8 Find out where the parents will be while they are out and all the necessary information regarding those locations, such as addresses and phone numbers. Ask the parents for a specific call list of whom to call first in an emergency if they cannot be reached.

9 Get comfortable with all the household rules and traditions.

10 Keep safety in mind at all times with the children, the house, and yourself.

11 Always locate a first aid kit or related medical supplies in the home in which you are babysitting.

12 Consider learning CPR and the Heimlich manoeuvre ahead of time, as these techniques could save a life in an emergency situation.

13 Avoid water-related activities if at all possible, and only bathe a child if a parent has asked you to do so.

14 Prevent misbehaviour by surrounding children with a positive environment.

15 Understanding children's levels of development will help you make better choices when dealing with their behaviour.

16 Offer to help or tutor children with their homework. Parents will be impressed and extremely thankful because it will be one less thing they will have to do.

17 Try to follow the bedtime and mealtime routines as closely as possible.

18 Playing with the children you are babysitting is the best way to get to know them.

19 Come prepared with fun ideas for games and other activities to keep the children entertained and out of trouble.

20 Allow children to choose or make up their own games.

Further Information

You can find out more about babysitting through books, websites, and other resources. Here are some helpful places to start.

Websites

www.4children.org.uk
This website provides support for all children and young people in their local community.

www.connexions-direct.com
Connexions offers advice, support and information for 13–19 year olds.

www.dfes.gov.uk/youngpeople
Information, resources, and advice for young people.

www.babysittingclass.com
The babysitter's certificate class online trains sitters worldwide to prevent emergencies and give thoughtful, loving care to their charges.

www.campaigns.direct.gov.uk/firekills
Tips for avoiding fires at home and safety tips.

Books

365 Manners Kids Should Know: Games, Activities, and Other Fun Ways to Help Children Learn Etiquette, Sheryl Eberly (Three Rivers Press, 2001)

Amelia's Guide to Babysitting, Marissa Moss (Simon & Schuster, 2008)

Babysitting Activities: Fun with Kids of All Ages, Wendy Ann Mattox (Snap Books, 2006)

Babysitting Basics: Caring for Kids, Leah Browning (Snap Books, 2006)

British Medical Association A-Z Family Medical Encyclopedia (Dorling Kindersley 2004)

First Aid for Children Fast, Gordon Paterson (Dorling Kindersley, 2002)

Life Skills: Managing Money, Barbara Hollander (Heinemann Library, 2008)

Speak Up and Get Along! Learn The Mighty Might, Thought Chop, And More Tools To Make Friends, Stop Teasing, And Feel Good About Yourself, Scott Cooper (Free Spirit Publishing, 2005)

The Little Book of Good Behaviour, Christine Coirault (Frogillo Books, 2007)

The New Totally Awesome Business Book for Kids, Arthur and Rose Bochner (Newmarket, 2007)

The Pocket Guide to CPR for Infants and Children, Gloria Blatti (Pocket Books,1998)

What to Expect: Baby-Sitter and Nanny Handbook, Heidi Murkoff (Pocket Books, 2005)

ORGANISATIONS

www.redcross.org.uk
Check out which health and safety classes the Red Cross offers in your area.

www.rospa.com/safetyeducation/advice/babysitting.htm
This is the website for the Royal Society for the Prevention of Accidents, and it has useful information on babysitting.

Glossary

allergic being naturally affected in a bad way by a plant or food

ambition having energy for work and activity

authority someone who is in charge or command

certification official recognition that a person has met certain standards, such as taking a class in CPR

client customer or someone who receives the benefit of a service

coax attempt to gently persuade someone to do something

CPR abbreviation for "cardiopulmonary resuscitation," which is an emergency procedure performed on someone who has no pulse and has stopped breathing

empowerment feeling of power

evacuation leaving a dangerous situation in a planned way

hazard object or area that can be dangerous

Heimlich manoeuvre emergency rescue procedure performed on someone who is choking

impression judgement a person inspires about himself or herself when meeting someone else

incentive something that inspires someone to do something

instinct natural impulse that can cause a reaction or form an opinion

itinerary detailed path or plan

lucrative something that is profitable or that makes money

mould give shape and character to someone or something

nurture help the development of someone

overstimulated experiencing too many things all at once

possessive claiming ownership

profanity use of words that are considered bad or foul language

prospective someone or something that has the potential of being obtained

reference person who recommends others for a position of employment

referral written or spoken recommendation

reprimand disapprove of something in a formal way

reputation way a person is viewed by others

seminar course, meeting, or study

sterile very clean; free from germs and other micro-organisms

suffocate take away fresh air or prevent from breathing

verbal contract spoken agreement often made official by a handshake

Index